What Does a Nun Do?

by Susan Heyboer O'Keefe

illustrations by H. M. Alan

PAULIST PRESS
New York/Mahwah, N.J.

For Father Rob and Sister Pat—S.H.O'K.

Celebrate!—H.M.A.

Text and cover design by Lynn Else
Cover illustrations by H. M. Alan

Library of Congress Cataloging-in-Publication Data

O'Keefe, Susan Heyboer.
   What does a priest do? what does a nun do? / by Susan Heyboer O'Keefe.
     p. cm.
   Two stories bound back to back and inverted.
   Summary: One side of this upside-down book celebrates all of the things that priests do. Turning the book over and around produces a similar celebration of nuns.
   ISBN 0-8091-6698-4 (alk. paper)
   1. Upside-down books—Specimens. 2. Priests—Juvenile literature. 3. Nuns—Juvenile literature. [1. Priests. 2. Nuns. 3. Occupations. 4. Upside-down books.] I. Title.
BX1913 .O43 2001
270'.092'2—dc21

2001051025

Published by Paulist Press
997 Macarthur Boulevard
Mahwah, New Jersey 07430

www.paulistpress.com

Printed and bound in the
United States of America

She prays.

She helps the poor and the sick.

She teaches.

She listens to people's problems.

She laughs a lot,

and sometimes she cries.

She travels to faraway places,

and she lives right next door.

Some days her job is hard.

Other days her job is easy.

But *every* day her job is full of love, because she shares Jesus with the world.

prays helps teaches listens laughs cries shares loves

cries shares loves prays helps teaches listens laughs

But *every* day his job is full of love, because he shares Jesus with the world.

Some days his job is hard.

and he
lives right
next door.

He travels to faraway places,

and sometimes he cries.

He laughs a lot,

He listens to people's problems.

He teaches.

He helps the poor and the sick.

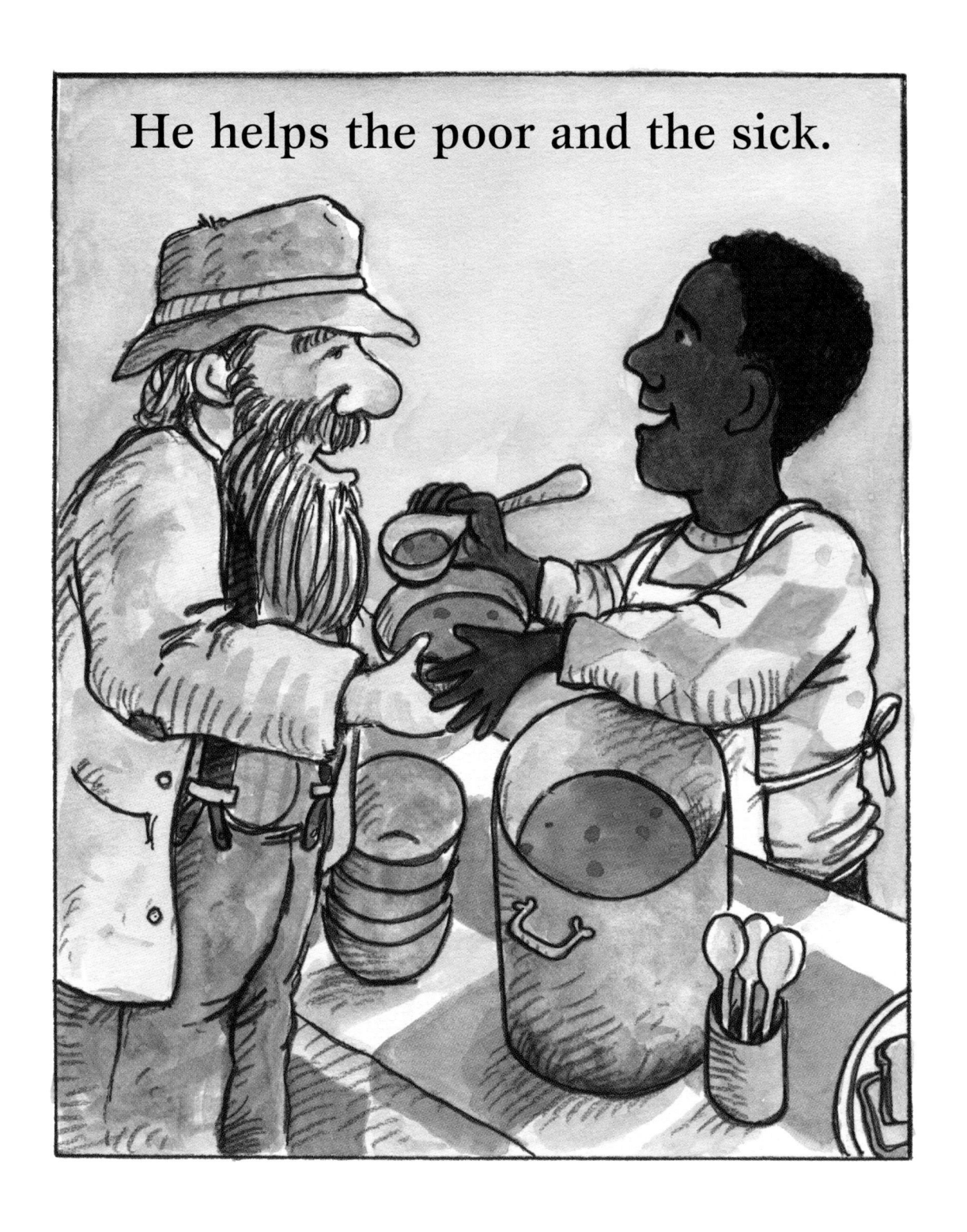

He prays.

A priest does all sorts of
interesting things.

For Father Rob and Sister Pat—S.H.O'K.

Celebrate!—H.M.A.

Text Copyright © 2002 by Susan Heyboer O'Keefe
Illustrations Copyright © 2002 by H. M. Alan

Text and cover design by Lynn Else
Cover illustrations by H. M. Alan

Library of Congress Cataloging-in-Publication Data

O'Keefe, Susan Heyboer.
    What does a priest do? what does a nun do? / by Susan Heyboer O'Keefe.
        p. cm.
    Two stories bound back to back and inverted.
    Summary: One side of this upside-down book celebrates all of the things that priests do. Turning the book over and around produces a similar celebration of nuns.
    ISBN 0-8091-6698-4 (alk. paper)
    1. Upside-down books—Specimens. 2. Priests—Juvenile literature. 3. Nuns—Juvenile literature. [1. Priests. 2. Nuns. 3. Occupations. 4. Upside-down books.] I. Title.
BX1913.O43 2001
270′.092′2—dc21
                                                            2001051025

Published by Paulist Press
997 Macarthur Boulevard
Mahwah, New Jersey 07430

www.paulistpress.com

Printed and bound in the
United States of America

What Does a
Priest Do?

by Susan Heyboer O'Keefe

illustrations by H. M. Alan

PAULIST PRESS
New York/Mahwah, N.J.